ideals® CHRISTMAS

God bless you all this Christmas Day;
may Bethlehem's star still light the way
and guide thee to the perfect peace
when every fear and doubt shall cease;
and may thy home such glory know
as did the stable long ago.
—EDGAR A. GUEST

NASHVILLE, TENNESSEE

The Things That Make It Christmas

Garnett Ann Schultz

The things that make it Christmas
are the million little joys:
the happiness and laughter
of the many girls and boys,
the holly in the window
and the tree so grand and tall,
the mistletoe that's hanging
so inviting in the hall.

The things that make it precious
are the eyes so shining bright
and the lovely sacred music
in the stillness of the night,
the pleasant decorations
and the snow so wondrous fair,
the little bits of giving
that are part of everywhere.

The things that make it special
are so little it would seem:
a package tied with ribbon
and a heart that holds a dream,
a box of Christmas cookies
for a neighbor 'cross the way,
the smell of roasting turkey
in the kitchen Christmas Day.

The things that make it Christmas
are just little bits of cheer,
and just little bits of gladness
we forget throughout the year—
no difference but the season
when our hearts have bigger grown.
The things that make it Christmas
are the things that bless each home.

CHRISTMAS by Marcello Corti. Image © Marcello Corti/Advocate Art

Poinsettias

J. Harold Gwynne

We hail you, lovely Christmas flower,
with scarlet petals bright.
How graciously you bear your name:
"The Flower of Holy Night!"

Your beauty takes the breath away
in fields of brilliant blooms,
in gaily planted garden plots,
in quiet living rooms.

But most of all, in every church,
with chancel all aglow,
you thrill the hearts of worshippers
and wondrous beauty show.

You symbolize for all of us
the hopes of Christmas Day;
you decorate our gifts of love
and brighten all our way.

Repeat the message that we need,
dear Flower of Holy Night;
remind us of the Savior's love
and keep us in His light.

A Poinsettia for You

Estelle Williams

The Christmas flower is glowing bright
in house and garden everywhere,
lending color to the earth
and magic to the air.

I hope the flower of joy unfolds
like this poinsettia, with art,
and lights with singing, mystic flame
each corner of your heart.

Image © marilyn barbone/Shutterstock

Christmas
Author Unknown

God gave us hills,
white hills in the moonlight;
lacy gray shadows
that quiver and run;
and light, fluffy snowflakes
that drift in the dusk
to a world veiled in stillness
as night is begun.

God gave us waters,
ice-bound and frozen.
God gave us little white
tracks in the snow;
and little, fat sparrows
that sleep in the
　　　church-tops;
and bells that peal out
to the stillness below.

God gave us Christmas
and bright wreaths
　　　of holly;
taught us, like Jesus,
to bless and forgive.
He tilled all our hearts
with that peace universal.
God gave us love
and the spirit to give.

Crater Lake and Wizard Island in winter,
Crater Lake National Park, Oregon.
Photograph © Stock Connection/SuperStock.

The Christmas Ribbon

Dona Maxey

It was early December. All over town, lights glistened jewel-like across snowy yards. Even stores wore garlands of silver and gold. My parents were visiting, and because we would not be together for Christmas, Mother wanted to celebrate early with the children.

"Let's put up the tree," she urged with a festive air.

"Yes!" agreed the children, exuberant.

The day after Thanksgiving would not have been too early for them to start decorating, but somehow, Christmas had snuck up on me. I was not ready for it. I figured we'd decorate later this year. That would give me a chance to get into the Christmas spirit.

But here was Mother, whose eyes beseeched while the children danced around, pleading. I thought, *Who am I to stand in the way of grandmotherly satisfaction?*, and I surrendered.

While my mother and children, cheerfully immersed in Christmas glee, decorated the tree in the front room, I puttered around listlessly, halfheartedly decorating the rest of the house. I held a silky snip of green ribbon and looked vaguely around for something to tie it onto. I choose a perfume bottle on my dresser, but even as I knotted a festive bow, I began to sigh inwardly. *The last thing I want to do is tie ribbon around little bottles. This is dumb. How did I get roped into this?*

With a jolt, I looked up and stared in the mirror. *Dumb? You are tying this ribbon because Jesus came! You would decorate for anyone else's birthday party. Why not for His?* My wide eyes looked past the image in the mirror, and I imagined lights glimmering on houses and stores and schools around the world. I saw humble crèches and glitter and tinsel and colorful ribbons fastened everywhere. I heard carols pealing from a million radios and stereos and PA systems.

It's a party! I mused joyfully. I couldn't help smiling. *All over the world, people are celebrating the birth of our Lord!*

"Fear not: for, behold, I bring you good tidings of great joy, which shall be to all people," announced the angel to the shepherds on that day long ago. And the answering chorus chanted, "Glory to God in the highest, and on earth peace, good will toward men" (Luke 2:10, 14 KJV). A birthday announcement if ever there was one.

I looked back at the perfume bottle and straightened my bow. Suddenly, bells were ringing and carols were playing in my heart. It was Christmas!

Image © GAP Photos

For It's Christmas, You Know
George J. Makris

The sound of carol-singing,
children shouting out with glee,
the church bells with their joyous ringing—
that's what Christmas means to me.

The sound of happy voices
as folks rush to and fro.
The whole world on this day rejoices
for it's Christmastime, you know!

'Twas on this day, remember,
o'er two thousand years ago,
a clear blue sky in cold December
brought the message we all know.

By radiant light we're blinded,
falling to our knees to pray,
and only then are we reminded
that today is Christmas Day.

Christmas Season
Lucille Veneklasen

A season of gladness
for young and for old,
of music, of laughter,
of stories retold.

A season of beauty,
a season of zest,
of friendships renewed
and of kindness expressed.

A season of love
and of wide-spreading cheer,
a season of hope
for the newest New Year.

A season of worship,
of carols resung,
a season of blessing
for old and for young.

Image © iStock.com/Lisa Thornberg

The Sharing Tree
Louise Pugh Corder

What stately indoor Christmas tree,
with baubles all aglow,
can equal our great living pine
that stands out in the snow?

The boughs are decked with suet balls
and draped with popcorn chains.
Big peanut-buttered pinecones hang
among the sheaves of grain.

The brilliant, plumaged ornaments
that perch upon this tree,
created by the Master's hand,
show great variety.

Bright cardinals lend rich scarlet hues,
the jays their vivid blue.
The grosbeaks, towhees, chickadees
are gems of beauty too.

When Christmastime is long since past
and presents put away,
our outdoor tree will offer treats
to feathered friends each day.

After the Snowfall
Clay Harrison

The day after a snowfall,
the sky's a bluer blue.
The air seems crisper than before;
the sun is brighter too.
These are picture-perfect days
as seasons come and go;
there's nothing quite as awesome
as the freshly fallen snow.

The cardinals at my feeders
are a lovely sight to see.
They look like decorations
on a snow-capped cedar tree.
The snow's a sea of diamonds
underneath the morning sun;
engulfed in purple shadows
just before the day is done.

Sometimes the snow stays longer
when the temperatures are low
to make a winter wonderland
before it has to go.
How children love their snow days,
for they never mind the cold;
such days are precious memories
we'll treasure when we're old.

Image © Masterfile

Bits & Pieces

*C*hristmas is not a time nor a season, but a state of mind. To cherish peace and goodwill, to be plenteous in mercy, is to have the real spirit of Christmas.

—*Calvin Coolidge*

*C*hristmas is a day of meaning and traditions, a special day spent in the warm circle of family and friends.

—*Margaret Thatcher*

*O*ur hearts grow tender with childhood memories and love of kindred, and we are better throughout the year for having, in spirit, become a child again at Christmastime.
—*Laura Ingalls Wilder*

A little smile, a word of cheer,
a bit of love from someone near,
a little gift from one held dear,
best wishes for the coming year:
these make a merry Christmas!
—*John Greenleaf Whittier*

*M*y idea of Christmas, whether old-fashioned or modern, is very simple: loving others. Come to think of it, why do we have to wait for Christmas to do that?
—*Bob Hope*

*T*he rooms were very still while the pages were softly turned and the winter sunshine crept in to touch the bright heads and serious faces with a Christmas greeting.
—*Louisa May Alcott,* LITTLE WOMEN

Surprised and Delighted

Lindsey Smallwood

I had no idea it was coming. This speaks to my mom's cleverness, because I was a notorious present-peeker. Unwrapping packages without ripping the paper was my specialty. Each year I spent hours stealthily surveying the gifts under our tree, carefully pulling back the tape to discover what was inside and building a mental inventory of who was getting what. By the time we read the Nativity story on Christmas Eve, I usually had every box accounted for.

But not that year. I was ten years old, and as we opened our presents, I knew the contents of each package with my name on it—a new dress, some socks and underwear, a set of books I couldn't wait to dive into. We had nearly finished exchanging gifts when my mom reached behind her rocking chair and pulled out a narrow package. She handed the package to me, smiling as I shook the box, confused, wondering at its contents.

Stumped, I tore off the paper and gasped when I saw what was inside. It was a phone—a landline phone for my bedroom. My very own extension! It was made of neon foam, with an oversized yellow ear at the top and giant hot pink lips serving as the mouthpiece. I saw myself lying on my bed and having private talks with friends from school, like the cool girls in the books I adored. I was completely surprised and delighted! It was the perfect gift I never expected—a sign that my mom knew me and what I would love, even before I thought to ask for it.

As I recall *this* Christmas story, I'm struck that it is also *the* Christmas story. As Jesus reminds us in the Gospel of Matthew, ". . . your Father knows what you need before you ask Him" (Matthew 6:8, ESV). We think we know what's coming, and then God delivers a surprise.

We would never think to ask for a baby born in poverty to an unwed mother, but the Incarnation is exactly what we've always longed for. It's the reality of God loving us enough to enter into our experience. The gift of Christ's coming in the Christmas story is evidence that God knows us, understands us, and has been planning to delight us all along. Jesus is everything we want and yet more than we knew to ask for, the way good presents usually are.

Image © GAP Photos/Douglas Gibb

Through My Window

The Trail of Tradition

Pamela Kennedy

Christmas is my favorite time of year. I enjoy the lights and the cookies, the tree and the candles. I love the beautiful story of how God came to make his home with us on a starry night two millennia ago and how He still remains within those who love Him. But I also treasure the traditions of generations come and gone and of those that will carry on. This trail of family tradition winding through the years leads me from Christmases long ago toward Christmases yet to be.

When my husband and I married, we united some of our families' holiday customs and added our own to create our unique take on the season. I learned to make his mother's Julekake, a yeasty sweetbread laden with fruit and nuts, frosted with almond glaze. He, in turn, adapted to my mother's "roast beast" as our holiday main course. We still serve the savory prime rib crusted with pepper and garlic on my great-grandmother's oval Furnivals platter!

Early in our marriage, on a visit to Hong Kong, we purchased several dozen small silk embroidered animals that we have hung on our tree for over forty Christmases. And at a post-holiday sale one year, I got a great deal on a Nativity set because one of the shepherds was missing an arm. I couldn't throw him out, so every year he still stands with the Holy Family, somewhat lopsided, beside the Babe in the manger. It just wouldn't be Christmas without him!

Once our children came along, they added their own special traditions to our Christmas trail. When our oldest son was a preschooler in Hawaii, he crafted a diminutive wreath ornament from a wooden drapery loop coated with glue, rolled in sand, and accented with tiny shells from the beach. He's forty now, but every time I hang that ornament on the tree I see his four-year-old eyes shining with pride. And when we drive past houses adorned with Christmas lights, I hear my young daughter's hopeful question, "We'll still have time to look at lights after the candlelight service, right, Mom?" She's in her thirties now, but on Christmas Eve I still see her in pigtails.

As my children marry and establish their families, they create new Christmas memories, blending bits and pieces of their spouses' traditions with their own. Our younger son, his wife, and their two little ones traipse into the woods in early December to choose their tree. Then they bring it home to decorate with homemade strings of cranberries and paper stars trimmed with glit-

Photograph by © Pixel Stories/Stocksy

ter glue. My three-year-old grandson points out the duckling ornament his Nana sent when he was "just a little kid," while his baby sister gazes with infant eyes at the colored lights. They are enhancing the family trail bit by bit, creating Christmas memories they will carry on for decades.

This past December in Chicago, my daughter and her husband, expecting their first child, combed through frigid parking lots filled with half-frozen firs to find the perfect tree. Hauling it up two flights of stairs with hands numb from the cold, they quickly placed it in the tree stand, then admired their find while clasping steaming cups of tea to defrost their fingers. Afterward, they carefully hung ornaments garnered from their world travels, creating a tableau of their first five years together, and dreamt about a little boy who will join them for his first Christmas this year.

As I arrange our Nativity set again this December, I tuck a few sprigs of holly around the broken shepherd and contemplate the trail of our family holidays. I smile, realizing again the treasure of family and the truth that we never walk this path alone. Past travelers, those with us now, and generations yet to be all join together in the traditions of our Christmases.

Going Home

LaVerne P. Larson

I'm going home for Christmas,
to that lovely place aglow
with a special magic splendor
I have always treasured so.

I'm going home for Christmas,
to where love waits at the door,
and my heart is ever welcome
to share happiness in store.

I'm going home for Christmas,
far across the sparkling snow,

to hear stories, bells, and carols,
and to bask in candleglow.

I'm going home for Christmas
where I'll trim the Christmas tree
and give gifts to all my loved ones,
for they mean the world to me.

I'm going home for Christmas
because I love it there.
My home is heaven here on earth
with blessings I may share.

WINTER-HOUSE *by Marcello Corti.*
Image © Marcello Corti/Advocate Art.

When Mom Made Christmas

Ellen Carter Clark

Cynthia sits atop a shelf now. Her hair is a little thinner for the efforts of her nine-year-old beautician, and her left arm bears a small incision, evidence of a repair by my father, the doll surgeon. But her eyes still shine bright with the reflections of fifty-nine Christmases. Like Dickens's Spirit of Christmas Past, Cynthia serves to remind me of the glorious yuletides of my youth.

My mind drifts back to 1957, to our little three-room house in the foothills of Appalachia. We had no bathroom, no running water, and no telephone; and I slept on a portable fold-away contraption that converted our living room into my bedroom at night.

The advantage of a small house was this: hearing in great detail all the wonderful rustling and readying of my parents as they "made Christmas" every Christmas Eve. Because of my place on the roll-away bed, I had the honor of sleeping beside the Christmas tree. It is a place I long for to this day! Even now, on Christmas Eve, when the rest of the family has long since drifted in slumber toward another Christmas morn, I lie down by the tree for just a little while, keeping vigil as in 1957. I think part of me is waiting, longing to hear the hushed noises of Mom wrapping packages and Dad attaching the legs to a dolly tea table.

When I woke at dawn on that Christmas Day fifty-nine years ago, my eyes surveyed our rotund Norway spruce, which nearly touched the ceiling of our tiny house. Reused tinsel icicles glistened merrily in great clumps. In the glow of the colored electric Christmas tree bulbs—huge by today's standards—and Dad's favorite bubble lights, I caught the gleam of Cynthia's eyes. My heart raced!

A grown-up lady doll, Cynthia sat on one of two child-sized pink chairs at a small Formica tea table. Her midnight blue, pin-dotted taffeta party dress billowed about her, and an elegant string of tiny pearls encircled her neck. A quick appraisal further revealed, to my delight, real seamed nylon stockings and shiny black high heels with elastic straps across the toes. And finally, reflecting Mom's keen sense of detail, Cynthia's curly strawberry blonde hair was the exact color of my own. How perfectly beautiful she was!

Other toys accompanied my new doll under the tree that Christmas, but Cynthia, with her jointed knees and sleep eyes, quickly became my constant companion. My earliest sewing efforts resulted in her one-of-a-kind wardrobe. She was the last doll of my childhood, but she lasted far beyond it.

I have never thought of our family as poor. But now, recalling my early years in the three-room house, I understand we were only wealthy because of my mother's resourcefulness and sacrifices. Did she wear her Sunday dress another year, or do without new twelve-dollar linoleum to buy Cynthia? I wouldn't be surprised if it were so. And as I smile at my treasured doll on yet another Christmas Eve, I am filled with gratitude for my mother's tireless work to "make Christmas" for her family.

Image © Jaroslaw Pawlak/Shutterstock

The Balsam Wood Cabin

Andrew L. Luna

Over the years when I was a child, my mother would add some items to the Christmas village which was always perched bravely atop the old antique pedestal desk in our living room. Occasionally, she would add a tree or two, create a new pond from a piece of mirror, or add some new figurines of people or animals frolicking in the soft white snow made of cotton and glitter. One year, she ingeniously created a small aluminum-foil stream, flowing into the town from the mountain we made by stacking together atlases and smaller books.

One December day, I opened a package to discover that Mom had bought a real balsam wood cabin. It was very lightweight, about four inches by four inches in size, and it had one door opening in the center. This cabin fascinated me immensely.

The cabin's roof could be removed to allow a burner with incense to be placed inside and lighted. The cabin came with a package of twelve incense cones that smelled of evergreen. The true magic of the cabin was soon revealed when the incense was ignited and the roof was placed back on the structure. In a matter of seconds, smoke would rise up from its chimney and hover over the little village, filling the entire living room with that heavenly aroma.

The look, feel, and smell of that log cabin was so woodsy and real, despite its location within our artificial village. It brought to mind the faint call of a lone wolf from within distant pines, the haunting cry of a loon as he flew gracefully over a dark lake, or the sound of the icy wind slicing its way down to the villagers preparing for Christmas. Every time I looked at that cabin, aided by the stories I had read, I thought of fantastic adventures in a far-off wilderness. It was the modest homestead of Daniel Boone as he helped tame the rugged territory of Kentucky. I looked around the cabin to see if Buck the dog, from Jack London's *Call of the Wild*, was patiently waiting outside for his master to come out and hook up the team. I even remembered some Henry David Thoreau excerpts read by my English teacher, and I thought of his cabin on Walden Pond. Inspired, I picked up our balsam wood cabin, moved it out by the large mirrored lake, and waited for ole Henry to come out of his warm cabin to fish for his dinner.

From that point forward, Christmas would never be complete without the smell of evergreen incense and the little puffs of white smoke billowing from the chimney of the little cabin. As the years progressed, our Christmas village got

Photograph © Stuart Dee/The Image Bank/Getty Images

more elaborate and fancy. New porcelain homes replaced the tired, tattered cardboard ones. Plastic snow replaced the cotton, and new lighting technology allowed for more creativity. However, I always made sure that our balsam wood cabin was placed next to the big mirror-pond, where its smoke and its memories could be enjoyed by all.

Though my mom doesn't put up the village or the cabin anymore, its memory is tucked gently away in my mind. All that's needed to remind me is the smell of evergreen incense. That aroma rekindles memories of holidays past, when a little balsam wood cabin ignited the imagination of a young boy at Christmastime.

*Gifts of time and love
are surely the basic ingredients
of a truly merry Christmas.*
—Peg Bracken

Advent Wreath Aglow

Pamela Love

An island of light
in the darkness serene;
candles like stars
on a wreath evergreen.

Together these flames
turn into one glow,
like one round a manger
so long, long ago.

A Christmas Wreath

Ruth Gower

I'm sending you a
    Christmas wreath
to hang up in your heart.
It's evergreen and shining,
friendship's perfect
    work of art,
with little thorns of memory
to catch and hold
    the thought,

and cones of hope and
    laughter berries
in its twinings wrought.
Its perfect roundness
    tells a tale
of love that lasts unbroken.
Our hearts hold Christmas
    all year round—
of this my wreath's the token.

Image © GAP Photos/Friedrich Strauss

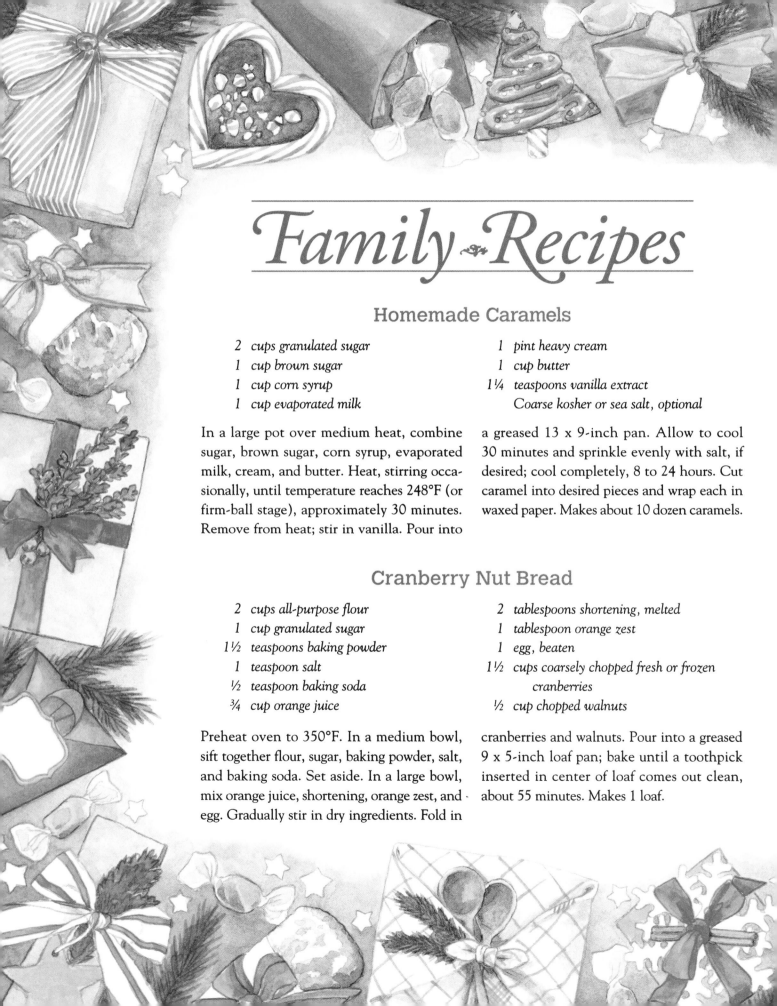

Family Recipes

Homemade Caramels

2 cups granulated sugar
1 cup brown sugar
1 cup corn syrup
1 cup evaporated milk

1 pint heavy cream
1 cup butter
1¼ teaspoons vanilla extract
Coarse kosher or sea salt, optional

In a large pot over medium heat, combine sugar, brown sugar, corn syrup, evaporated milk, cream, and butter. Heat, stirring occasionally, until temperature reaches 248°F (or firm-ball stage), approximately 30 minutes. Remove from heat; stir in vanilla. Pour into a greased 13 x 9-inch pan. Allow to cool 30 minutes and sprinkle evenly with salt, if desired; cool completely, 8 to 24 hours. Cut caramel into desired pieces and wrap each in waxed paper. Makes about 10 dozen caramels.

Cranberry Nut Bread

2 cups all-purpose flour
1 cup granulated sugar
1½ teaspoons baking powder
1 teaspoon salt
½ teaspoon baking soda
¾ cup orange juice

2 tablespoons shortening, melted
1 tablespoon orange zest
1 egg, beaten
1½ cups coarsely chopped fresh or frozen cranberries
½ cup chopped walnuts

Preheat oven to 350°F. In a medium bowl, sift together flour, sugar, baking powder, salt, and baking soda. Set aside. In a large bowl, mix orange juice, shortening, orange zest, and egg. Gradually stir in dry ingredients. Fold in cranberries and walnuts. Pour into a greased 9 x 5-inch loaf pan; bake until a toothpick inserted in center of loaf comes out clean, about 55 minutes. Makes 1 loaf.

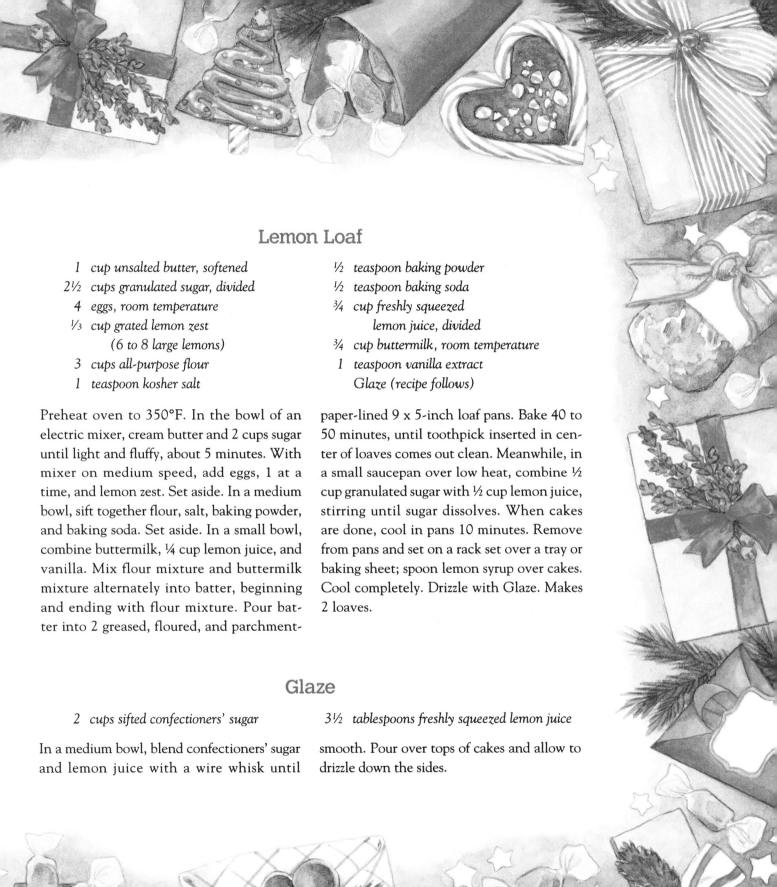

Lemon Loaf

1 cup unsalted butter, softened	½ teaspoon baking powder
2½ cups granulated sugar, divided	½ teaspoon baking soda
4 eggs, room temperature	¾ cup freshly squeezed
⅓ cup grated lemon zest	lemon juice, divided
(6 to 8 large lemons)	¾ cup buttermilk, room temperature
3 cups all-purpose flour	1 teaspoon vanilla extract
1 teaspoon kosher salt	Glaze (recipe follows)

Preheat oven to 350°F. In the bowl of an electric mixer, cream butter and 2 cups sugar until light and fluffy, about 5 minutes. With mixer on medium speed, add eggs, 1 at a time, and lemon zest. Set aside. In a medium bowl, sift together flour, salt, baking powder, and baking soda. Set aside. In a small bowl, combine buttermilk, ¼ cup lemon juice, and vanilla. Mix flour mixture and buttermilk mixture alternately into batter, beginning and ending with flour mixture. Pour batter into 2 greased, floured, and parchment-paper-lined 9 x 5-inch loaf pans. Bake 40 to 50 minutes, until toothpick inserted in center of loaves comes out clean. Meanwhile, in a small saucepan over low heat, combine ½ cup granulated sugar with ½ cup lemon juice, stirring until sugar dissolves. When cakes are done, cool in pans 10 minutes. Remove from pans and set on a rack set over a tray or baking sheet; spoon lemon syrup over cakes. Cool completely. Drizzle with Glaze. Makes 2 loaves.

Glaze

2 cups sifted confectioners' sugar	3½ tablespoons freshly squeezed lemon juice

In a medium bowl, blend confectioners' sugar and lemon juice with a wire whisk until smooth. Pour over tops of cakes and allow to drizzle down the sides.

Babyproof

Anne Kennedy Brady

The tree is decorated and tiny sparkling lights adorn the doorway. Carefully I unwrap the Nativity set and begin arranging the small painted statues. I've always been drawn to the Magi, and as a small child I would line them up clear across the room from the manger, imagining their ancient trek. This year, however, my thoughts turn to Mary as I nestle her beside the manger. I have always admired her, but having recently given birth to my first child, I feel something different this year: kinship. Despite the centuries that separate our experiences—and of course the distinction of her Divine Son—I wonder if our journeys to motherhood share more similarities than differences.

When my husband and I shared our news with friends and family over the holidays last year, those with young children were especially excited to welcome us to the club. Along with the deluge of baby-related Christmas gifts came recommendations of favorite books, websites, and smartphone apps promising to help us navigate this brave new world. Everyone had an opinion about how to care for our baby, who at that point was roughly the size of a kumquat.

I thought of our Lord's mother, young and afraid, longing for direction to raise this important Child. Did her mother pass on advice from her own experience? Did she have friends who touted the latest fads? Certainly there were fewer competing childcare opinions than in today's world, but it doesn't mean she knew what she was getting into.

The first decision my husband and I faced was who would deliver our baby. We visited several practitioners, and I agonized over whom I would trust to welcome our child into this world. One couple we know swore by the doula they'd hired to get through natural childbirth in their home, while others praised the twin miracles of pain medication and well-staffed hospitals. I longed for simpler days when such decisions would have been made for me. And yet, I'm sure Mary would have appreciated a few more options when faced with an emergency birth in a stable, with only Joseph and a few animals in attendance!

Next, I considered my new diet. Mary likely ate what she and her fellow villagers were able to raise or grow. She probably spent less time than I worrying about added hormones or food allergies, but I'm sure we shared the burden of cravings. I made regular stops at the closest Chinese takeout restaurant. Mary may have sneaked extra helpings of lentil stew, or whatever settled her stomach that day. And while I double-checked to make sure all my cheese was pasteurized, I wonder if Mary shared similar worries—perhaps cooking the lamb just a little longer or giving the figs an extra wash.

Finally I began researching what I would need to know after the baby's arrival. While doing some early shopping, I found an adorable onesie sporting a tag proclaiming it fire-resistant. *Do babies spontaneously combust?* I wondered. Again I thought of Mary, wrapping her Newborn in swaddling clothing because that was all that was available to her. I wondered if the shepherds scolded her for not using a finer quality of wool (maybe something flame-retardant), or if perhaps the innkeepers had given her the swaddling clothes that they had used for their own children. I looked at the onesie again and my eyes filled with tears. I'm willing to bet she was just grateful to have her Son finally, safely in her arms.

In Sunday School, I learned that Mary was likely afraid after accepting the angel's news. And it makes sense—who wouldn't be frightened at the prospect of raising God's Son, not to mention breaking the news to her fiancé? But along with that, I think there is a universal fear that every mother feels, whether she's Mary, or whether she's just me. What will life be like with this new person in the world? And how will we handle it all?

When I was just over seven months pregnant, my parents visited us in Chicago. One night I came home from work to the heavenly scent of Mom's lasagna. Collapsing on the couch, I lamented that I wouldn't be able to eat a good, home-cooked meal again for years, as visions of boxed macaroni and cheese danced in my head. But Mom put her arm around me and pulled me in for a tight hug. Then she took me through the simple recipe and told me how best to freeze leftovers for easy, delicious weeknight dinners. I dried a few tears and hugged her back. Mary rose to mind again, sitting alone with Joseph and their new Son in the stable. As we joined hands around the dinner table that night, I hoped that Mary had found her own support system, too, in that little town of Bethlehem.

I sit back and admire my Nativity scene. A new baby makes travel tricky this Christmas, so family may have to come this direction instead. And while I can't promise a spotless house or a perfectly sleep-trained baby, I can promise a delicious meal that will fill the house with warmth and bring everyone together to celebrate new life. I think Mary would approve.

Easy Lasagna

9 wide lasagna noodles, uncooked
1 pound ground turkey or beef
1 24-ounce can traditional pasta sauce
¾ cup water
3 eggs, slightly beaten

3 cup cottage cheese
3 cup grated mozzarella cheese
½ cup grated Parmesan cheese,
        plus extra for topping
1 to 2 teaspoons Italian herbs (optional)

Preheat oven to 350°F. In a large skillet over medium-high heat, brown meat; drain. Add sauce and water, mixing until well combined. Remove from heat and set aside. In a large bowl, combine eggs, cheeses, and herbs. In a 13 x 9-inch pan, spoon just enough of the meat sauce mixture to cover the bottom—about ½ to 1 cup. Place 3 uncooked noodles on the sauce. Layer remaining ingredients in following order: ½ of the cheese mixture, ⅓ remaining meat sauce, 3 noodles, remaining cheese mixture, ½ remaining meat sauce, 3 noodles, and remaining meat sauce, making sure all noodles are wet. Sprinkle additional Parmesan cheese on top. Cover pan with foil. Bake 1 hour; remove foil and bake an additional 15 minutes. Remove from oven and let stand at least 10 minutes before serving. Makes 8 to 12 servings.

Christmas Moments

Eileen Spinelli

A man tying a fir tree
atop his snowy car.
A woman showing a child how
to craft a silver star.
A guitarist in a doorway
playing "Silent Night."
An alley—usually darkened—
awash in twinkling light.
Bright chatter at the bus stop.
A stranger's kind hello.
The candle-scent of evergreen.
A chapel's welcome glow.
How simple are the moments
that wintry hearts
love so.

Each sight, each sound
of Christmas
and fragrances sublime
make hearts and faces happy
this glorious Christmastime.
—CARICE WILLIAMS

Image © GAP Photos/Friedrich Strauss

The Little White Church

Rose Marie Overman

Starlight illumines the little white church
in a peace-loving valley beside a bright stream.
The steeple cross sparkles with radiant gold
in the light of the stars and a yellow moonbeam.

The magic of singing is heard in the air:
not grand alleluias of great city choirs,
but simpler strains that ascend from the soul,
resounding with sweetness that thrills and inspires.

Peace and contentment steal through the soft light
into the church and to all who believe
in the virtue of goodness, the power of faith,
the beauty and sacredness of Christmas Eve.

Help us, dear Father, to build in our hearts
a little white church bathed in tranquil moonlight,
where we may find solace, contentment, and joy,
not only at Christmas but all through the night.

*First Baptist Church and Gazebo on the Green in
Bristol, Vermont. Image © Andre Jenny/Mira.com*

Joseph

Grace Noll Crowell

How weary and how tired they must have been,
from Nazareth walking, since the day's pale start.
Joseph, with great responsibility;
Young Mary, with earth's Savior 'neath her heart.
They neared the village at the set of sun;
the man must hasten for a place to rest.
He watched the woman, grave, with anxious eyes,
and saw her clutch a white hand to her breast.

Was she too weary? Had they come too far?
He could not fail this gentle, precious one.
But now the crowded inn, the words, "No room,"
for Mary, soon to mother God's dear Son!
Joseph's heart was troubled. Could there be
no place in all this throng for them to go?
Then suddenly the stable, and a hand
that bade them enter. God had planned it so!

Image © Alexander Hoffmann/Shutterstock

Glory to God
Lola Neff Merritt

All the hills were ringing
on that bright Judean night,
with choirs of angels singing
in a burst of heavenly light.

"Glory to God in the highest!"
spoke the angel, soft and clear.
"Open your hearts,
   O men of earth,
for lo, God's Son is here!"

Angels' Wings
Pamela Love

An angel opened up his wings
to hover in the sky.
He told the startled shepherds
of a Babe who slept nearby.

And then a crowd of angels bright
appeared with wings outspread.
They filled the air with songs of praise
above the shepherds' heads.

And when at last the news was told,
on wings that brightly shone,
the angels soared with joyful hearts
back to their heavenly home.

Holy Night
Olive Weaver Ridenour

It must have been a night like this,
so starry-bright and still,
when shepherds heard an angel-choir
sing, "Peace: to men, good will!"
and, wondering, went to Bethlehem
to find, upon the hay,
Christ Jesus, little Babe divine,
on that first Christmas Day.

It must have been a night like this
when Mary, with a start,
heard strange tales that the shepherds told,
and "pondered in her heart."
The angels sing; the star still shines;
a pilgrim once again,
I go to seek the living Christ
this night in Bethlehem.

ROCKEFELLER CENTER *by Bill Bell. Image © Bill Bell/Art Licensing*

FEAR NOT, MARY AND JOSEPH

Luke 1:30–35, Matthew 1:18–25

And the angel said unto her, Fear not, Mary: for thou hast found favour with God. And, behold, thou shalt conceive in thy womb, and bring forth a son, and shalt call his name JESUS. He shall be great, and shall be called the Son of the Highest: and the Lord God shall give unto him the throne of his father David: And he shall reign over the house of Jacob for ever; and of his kingdom there shall be no end.

Then said Mary unto the angel, How shall this be, seeing I know not a man?

And the angel answered and said unto her, The Holy Ghost shall come upon thee, and the power of the Highest shall overshadow thee: therefore also that holy thing which shall be born of thee shall be called the Son of God.

Now the birth of Jesus Christ was on this wise: When as his mother Mary was espoused to Joseph, before they came together, she was found with child of the Holy Ghost.

Then Joseph her husband, being a just man, and not willing to make her a public example, was minded to put her away privily.

But while he thought on these things, behold, the angel of the LORD appeared unto him in a dream, saying, Joseph, thou son of David, fear not to take unto thee Mary thy wife: for that which is conceived in her is of the Holy Ghost. And she shall bring forth a son, and thou shalt call his name JESUS: for he shall save his people from their sins.

Now all this was done, that it might be fulfilled which was spoken of the Lord by the prophet, saying, Behold, a virgin shall be with child, and shall bring forth a son, and they shall call his name Emmanuel, which being interpreted is, God with us.

Then Joseph being raised from sleep did as the angel of the Lord had bidden him, and took unto him his wife: And knew her not till she had brought forth her firstborn son: and he called his name JESUS.

HOLY FAMILY *by Dona Gelsinger. Image ©
Dona Gelsinger/Gelsinger Licensing*

JESUS IS BORN IN A MANGER

Luke 2:1–12

And it came to pass in those days, that there went out a decree from Caesar Augustus that all the world should be taxed. (And this taxing was first made when Cyrenius was governor of Syria.) And all went to be taxed, every one into his own city.

And Joseph also went up from Galilee, out of the city of Nazareth, into Judaea, unto the city of David, which is called Bethlehem; (because he was of the house and lineage of David:) To be taxed with Mary his espoused wife, being great with child.

And so it was, that, while they were there, the days were accomplished that she should be delivered. And she brought forth her firstborn son, and wrapped him in swaddling clothes, and laid him in a manger; because there was no room for them in the inn.

And there were in the same country shepherds abiding in the field, keeping watch over their flock by night. And, lo, the angel of the Lord came upon them, and the glory of the Lord shone round about them: and they were sore afraid.

And the angel said unto them, Fear not: for, behold, I bring you good tidings of great joy, which shall be to all people. For unto you is born this day in the city of David a Saviour, which is Christ the Lord. And this shall be a sign unto you; Ye shall find the babe wrapped in swaddling clothes, lying in a manger.

SHEPHERDS AFIELD *by Dona Gelsinger. Image ©
Dona Gelsinger/Gelsinger Licensing*

HEROD AND THE WISE MEN

Matthew 2:1–15

Now when Jesus was born in Bethlehem of Judaea in the days of Herod the king, behold, there came wise men from the east to Jerusalem, Saying, Where is he that is born King of the Jews? for we have seen his star in the east, and are come to worship him.

When Herod the king had heard these things, he was troubled, and all Jerusalem with him. And when he had gathered all the chief priests and scribes of the people together, he demanded of them where Christ should be born.

And they said unto him, In Bethlehem of Judaea: for thus it is written by the prophet, And thou Bethlehem, in the land of Juda, art not the least among the princes of Juda: for out of thee shall come a Governor, that shall rule my people Israel.

Then Herod, when he had privily called the wise men, enquired of them diligently what time the star appeared. And he sent them to Bethlehem, and said, Go and search diligently for the young child; and when ye have found him, bring me word again, that I may come and worship him also.

When they had heard the king, they departed; and, lo, the star, which they saw in the east, went before them, till it came and stood over where the young child was. When they saw the star, they rejoiced with exceeding great joy.

And when they were come into the house, they saw the young child with Mary his mother, and fell down, and worshipped him: and when they had opened their treasures, they presented unto him gifts; gold, and frankincense and myrrh.

And being warned of God in a dream that they should not return to Herod, they departed into their own country another way.

And when they were departed, behold, the angel of the Lord appeareth to Joseph in a dream, saying, Arise, and take the young child and his mother, and flee into Egypt, and be thou there until I bring thee word: for Herod will seek the young child to destroy him.

When he arose, he took the young child and his mother by night, and departed into Egypt: And was there until the death of Herod: that it might be fulfilled which was spoken of the Lord by the prophet, saying, Out of Egypt have I called my son.

The Nativity *by Dona Gelsinger. Image ©
Dona Gelsinger/Gelsinger Licensing*

A Star Is Born

Glenda Collins Inman

A star was born in heaven
to announce the Savior's birth
to men who'd kept a faithful watch
below on weary earth.

This miracle had been foretold
by prophets long ago,
but many had not kept the watch,
and so they did not know.

God's works are still abundant
as He cares for every need;
His star of hope still brightly shines
to guide the ones who heed.

The miracle of love and peace
can be performed in you,
to give you joy this Christmas Day,
and each day all year through.

A Christmas Prayer

Glenda Collins Inman

In a lowly manger yon
in Bethlehem one night,
God's wondrous Gift was born to earth
beneath His guiding light.

Not many came to see the Babe
nor praised His humble birth,
nor realized that the love of God
had brought Him down to earth.

And as the Child grew to a Man,
He suffered shame and scorn.
We read of this and, filled with grief,
our hearts are drawn to mourn.

For even though He met despair
and grief on every hand,
we hear Him plea with sinful ones
to follow God's great plan.

And as He died upon the cross,
nailed there for me and you,
we hear Him pray to God, "Forgive,
they know not what they do."

What can I do in my poor life
to merit such a Friend,
who'll lead and guide me all the way
and save me in the end?

The answer's in His holy word,
a truth we all must face:
it can't be earned, it is a gift
of Christ's amazing grace.

So, as I welcome Christmas Day,
in my own heart shall be
an ever-thankful prayer to God,
that His Son died for me.

Image © iStock.com/cmfotoworks

Opening Night

Keith H. Graham

The night seemed like any other to the shepherds tending sheep in fields near Bethlehem. The air was fresh but uncomfortably cool. Sheep huddled together for warmth and protection. Unpredictable dangers lurked in the darkness.

Then, suddenly, everything changed. An angel sent from God appeared in the dark heavens and boldly announced the birth of Jesus Christ. As the shepherds trembled in their sandals, more angels joined the celebration. They sang heaven's praises, transforming the starry skies into a vast concert hall. It was opening night for a musical tradition of truth and beauty that continues to bless Christians today.

To conclude that I simply enjoy Christmas music would be both inaccurate and insufficient. I love it! I love the truth- and time-tested carols as well as new, creative compositions. I love the powerful sounds of a professional orchestra using both instruments and voices, first to captivate the audience and then move it to a standing ovation. I love to hear "Joy To The World" and "We Wish You A Merry Christmas" from the lips of sincere, shivering carolers on my front porch.

I love the resounding hallelujahs in the "Hallelujah Chorus" from Handel's *Messiah* just as much as the mellow sounds of silver and gold handbells on a wintry morning. The blended voices of a choir stirring up joy, peace, and hope in an auditorium decked out in reds, greens, and twinkling lights are the perfect complement to a snowy evening! And I delight in an unpredictable performance of "Away In A Manger" by wiggly, giggly children dressed as angels and shepherds—with perhaps a couple of wandering sheep headed for their proud parents' laps.

Every year, as soon as autumn leaves begin to fall, I eagerly begin listening to Christmas music on my daily walks. Each day's venture outdoors, no matter my destination, leads me straight back to a manger in Bethlehem, and the grand events surrounding the birth of Jesus—God's Son, and my Savior.

Opening night is over, but the concert it inspired and initiated continues uninterrupted. Christmas music heralds the greatest Gift of all, and I don't want to miss a single half note!

CHURCH CANDLES *by The Macneil Studio.*
Image © The Macneil Studio/Art Licensing

A Choir's Christmas

Pamela Love

We don't have angels' voices, Lord,
but we'll do all we can
to celebrate with sacred hymns
the Son of God and man.

Neither have we angels' wings
and so we ask that You
will help us reach all those we can
with joyous words, so true.

The Music of Christmas

Robin Ayscue

The melodies and music
of this joyous time of year,
make us long, O Savior sweet,
to draw Your presence near.

"Silent Night," that holy night,
we lift our hearts in praise.
To You who came to earth for us,
our grateful voice we raise.

"O Come, Let Us Adore Him" now,
let us proclaim Him King!
"It Came Upon A Midnight Clear,"
we reverently sing.

"O Little Town Of Bethlehem,"
if only you could know
that round your holy family,
a gentle wind doth blow.

It bears a glorious melody
upon its heavenly wings
that lifts our souls straight up to Him,
our Savior, King of kings.

"O Holy Night," the stars doth shine;
forever we will sing
the songs and sacred melodies
this season always brings.

*Image © Unicover Corp by arrangement with
Ansada Licensing Group, LLC*

The Story of a Song

A Carol for the Children

Pamela Kennedy

In 1865, Phillips Brooks, the well-loved pastor at Philadelphia's Holy Trinity Church, took an extended tour of the Holy Land. For almost a year, Rev. Brooks retraced the steps of Jesus and the Apostles. Then, on December 24, the young Episcopalian pastor rode on horseback from Jerusalem to Bethlehem to attend the Christmas Eve service held in Constantine's ancient basilica, built over the traditional site of the Nativity. During the services, which lasted from ten o'clock at night until three in the morning, Brooks was deeply moved as he listened to hymns of praise, scripture readings, and prayers. The vivid impressions from this Christmas Eve in Bethlehem would remain with him the rest of his life.

Returning to Philadelphia, Phillips Brooks again took up his responsibilities at Holy Trinity. Known as a man of great compassion and humility, Brooks was equally at home conferring with elderly congregants, counseling young couples, or even sitting on the floor reading Bible stories or playing blocks with the children from his Sunday school classes.

It was this love for his younger congregants that led him to pen the hauntingly beautiful Christmas carol, "O Little Town of Bethlehem." The children of the church were planning a Christmas program, and the reverend wanted to write a new Christmas song for them to sing. As he pondered the Nativity story one night, his thoughts drifted to his Christmas Eve in Bethlehem just a few years earlier. Recalling the beauty of the city, the darkness of the night, and the pageantry of the story, he quickly wrote four stanzas poetically interpreting his experience.

In the morning, Brooks gave his verses to the church organist, Lewis H. Redner, requesting that he compose a simple melody that the children could memorize for their program a few days later. Redner, an accomplished organist and composer, agreed, but then hit something of a writer's block. The night before the Christmas program he still had not come up with anything. Exhausted and distressed, Redner fell into bed and plunged into a deep sleep. Then, in the middle of the night, he started awake with the strains of a beautiful melody ringing in his ears. He hastily jotted down the notes, set them by his bedside, and went back to sleep. In the morning he completed the harmony for the inspired tune and taught it to the children.

That night, in December of 1868, the children of Philadelphia's Holy Trinity Church sang "O Little Town of Bethlehem." Nearly 150 years later, the simple melody and haunting lyrics continue to bless congregations around the world as they "proclaim the holy birth, and praises sing to God the King, and peace to men on earth!"

O Little Town of Bethlehem

Phillips Brooks (1835–1893)   Lewis H. Redner (1831–1908)

1. O lit - tle town of Beth - le - hem, How still we see thee lie!
2. For Christ is born of Ma - ry, And gath - ered all a - bove,
3. How si - lent - ly, how si - lent - ly The won - drous Gift is giv'n!
4. O ho - ly Child of Beth - le - hem, De - scend on us, we pray.

A - bove thy deep and dream - less sleep The si - lent stars go by;
While mor - tals sleep, the an - gels keep Their watch of won - d'ring love.
So God im - parts to hu - man hearts The bless - ings of His heav'n.
Cast out our sin, and en - ter in, Be born in us to - day.

Yet in thy dark streets shin - eth The ev - er - last - ing Light;
O morn - ing stars to - geth - er Pro - claim the ho - ly birth,
No ear may hear His com - ing, But in this world of sin,
We hear the Christ - mas an - gels The great glad tid - ings tell.

The hopes and fears of all the years Are met in thee to - night.
And prais - es sing to God the King, And peace to men on earth!
Where meek souls will re - ceive Him still, The dear Christ en - ters in.
O come to us, a - bide with us, Our Lord, Em - man - u - el.

Christmas Hope

Susan Sundwall

Lord Jesus, we can only hope
on this most glorious day,
that all who know
    Your endless love
will bow their heads and pray.

For You have touched
    our weary hearts
and called us to Your side
to worship at the manger stall
this lovely Christmastide.

A lowly infant once You were—
the Scriptures tell us so—

a Savior born of humble maid
two thousand years ago.

Your perfect birth
    in time and place
will cause us to recall
the promise of our Father
to reclaim us from the fall.

We bow our heads in thankfulness
this holy, blessed morn
and raise them up
    to tell the world
Salvation has been born.

Promise

Gloria R. Milbrath

Long centuries past,
a promise was made
that Jesus, the Savior,
would come as a babe.

And so it all happened
one deep, starlit night.
The Promise was born—
the true Christmas Light.

Image © Jeff Schultz/Alaska Stock—
Design Pics/SuperStock

Behold the Son!

Jean L. Croyle

In stark whitest snowfall, the cardinal so red
gathers straw pieces and flies to his bed.
High up in the pine tree, the blue jay calls out,
and nature continues with winter about.

The season of thanks, and of birth and salvation
must ne'er be forgotten. It's God's revelation!
His plan for mankind called for sacrifice, love,
which only could come from the One high above.

See snow gently falling upon children's faces;
they play, skate, and run to their favorite places.
Watch the world now embrace snow
and ice-covered hills,
and feel night's soft blankets dispel winter chills.

Thank God for this earth He created and styled
for all of His children. And when it grows mild,
then thank Him for blessings of beauty and grace,
the season's joys etched on your loved one's face.

Behold the calm stillness of winter's embrace.
Breathe in and slow down from the chaotic pace.
Take time to revel—enjoy what He's given—
His Son, born today, died for you and has risen!

Image © Myst/Adobe Stock

Homecoming Hearts

D. A. Hoover

At Christmastime when hearts are warm,
as sheltered from the winter storm,
we gather at our Christmas tree;
God's love is there, as meant to be.

Though filled with gifts,
  good food, and fun,
deep in the soul of every one

abides the Babe of Bethlehem,
down to the youngest one of them.

Though years bring change
  and paths will stray,
there shines that star each Christmas Day;
earth knows no paths mankind may roam
too far from memories of home.

Christmas Is the Miracle

Alice Mackenzie Swaim

Down the years of memory,
the pageant of Decembers,
Christmas is the miracle
that every heart remembers.

Above the dreaming little towns,
the fields of drifted snow,

there falls the benediction
of the Christmas star's warm glow.

And heavy hearts grow lighter,
and joyful voices ring,
to celebrate His birthday
and worship Christ, the King.

Photograph © Oredia Eurl/SuperStock

My Christmas Friend
Patricia Emme

The special joys of Christmas
are the ones we give and share:
the little smiles, the kindly deeds,
the words that say we care.

The special joys of Christmas
are the ones that we can send
to those who mean so much to us,
like you, my special friend.

Christmas Wish
Virginia Blanck Moore

May joy be yours
this Christmastime
and every day
    thereafter.
May health companion
you and yours,
and peace and love
    and laughter.

May every day
bring fresh delight
and fortune walk
    with you—
this is my wish
this Christmastime,
my friend, so dear
    and true.

Image © haveseen/Adobe Stock

A Christmas Wish

Henry Van Dyke

I am thinking of you today, because it is Christmas. And I wish you joy. And tomorrow, because it is the day after Christmas, I shall wish you joy. Mayhap I cannot tell you about it from day to day, for you may be far away, or we may be entangled with the things of life. But it makes no difference—my thoughts and my wishes will be with you. Whatever of joy or success comes to you, I shall be glad. Clear through the year, without pretense, I wish you the spirit of Christmas.

At Year's End

Glenda Collins Inman

As every year draws toward its close,
it's good to count the ways
that God has blessed and led us
through our nights and all our days.
For seldom can we understand,
until some time has passed,
how everything, placed in His hand,
worked for our good at last.
It warms and reassures us
to look back year after year,
for since He's led us in the past,
the future holds no fear.

Image © Wayne Bronson/Adobe Stock

Christmas Wishes

Letitia Morse Nash

Oh, Christmas is a time for love,
a time for tender giving,
a time for faith and hope and cheer,
a time for sweeter living,

a time to reach across the world
or just across the street,
a time to send good will afar
or give to those you meet.

And so I send you faith and hope,
good will and wishes true,
and add a special bit of love
I've saved for only you.

ISBN-13: 978-0-8249-1350-2

Published by Ideals
An imprint of Worthy Publishing Group
A division of Worthy Media, Inc.
Nashville, Tennessee

Copyright © 2016 by Worthy Media, Inc.

All rights reserved. No part of this publication may be reproduced or transmitted in any form or by any means, electronic or mechanical, including photocopy, recording, or any information storage and retrieval system, without permission in writing from the publisher.

Printed and bound in the U.S.A.
Printed on Weyerhauser Lynx. The paper used in this publication meets the minimum requirements of American National Standard for Information Sciences—Permanence of Paper for Printed Materials, ANSI Z39.48-1984.

Publisher, Peggy Schaefer
Editor, Melinda L. R. Rumbaugh
Permissions and Research, Kristi West
Copy Editors, Anne Kennedy Brady, Olivia Forehand
Designer, Marisa Jackson

Cover: *Victorian Seasons—Winter—Cardinal* by Susan Bourdet. Artwork courtesy of the artist and Wild Wings (800-445-4833, www.wildwings.com).
Inside front cover: *Christmas Shops* by Jim Mitchell. Image © Jim Mitchell/Advocate Art.
Inside back cover: *Carol Singers* by Jim Mitchell. Image © Jim Mitchell/Advocate Art.

Additional art credits: art for "Bits & Pieces," "Family Recipes," back cover spot art, and spot art for pages 1 and 52, by Kathryn Rusynyk. "O Little Town of Bethlehem" sheet music by Dick Torrans, Melode, Inc.

ACKNOWLEDGMENTS:

LUNA, ANDREW L. "The Balsam Wood Cabin" from *Unwrap the Memories* © Andrew Luna. All rights reserved. Used by permission. SMALLWOOD, LINDSEY. "Surprised and Delighted" from www.incourage.me. All rights reserved. Used by permission of the author. OUR THANKS to the following authors or their heirs: Robin Ayscue, Anne Kennedy Brady, Ellen Carter Clark, Louise Pugh Corder, Grace Noll Crowell, Jean L. Croyle, Patricia Emme, Ruth Gower, Keith H. Graham, Edgar A. Guest, J. Harold Gwynne, Clay Harrison, D. A. Hoover, Glenda Collins Inman, Pamela Kennedy, LaVerne P. Larson, Pamela Love, George J. Makris, Dona Maxey, Lola Neff Merritt, Gloria R. Milbrath, Virginia Blanck Moore, Letitia Morse Nash, Rose Marie Overman, Olive Weaver Ridenour, Garnett Ann Schultz, Eileen Spinelli, Susan Sundwall, Alice Mackenzie Swaim, Lucille Veneklasen, Estelle Williams.

Scripture quotations, unless otherwise indicated, are taken from King James Version (KJV). Scripture quotations marked ESV are taken from The Holy Bible, English Standard Version. Copyright © 2001 by Crossway, a publishing ministry of Good News Publishers. Used by permission. All rights reserved.

Every effort has been made to establish ownership and use of each selection in this book. If contacted, the publisher will be pleased to rectify any inadvertent errors or omissions in subsequent editions.

Join the community of *Ideals* readers on Facebook at: www.facebook.com/IdealsMagazine
Readers are invited to submit original poetry and prose for possible use in future publications. Please send no more than four typed submissions to: *Ideals* submissions, Worthy Publishing Group, 6100 Tower Circle, Suite 210, Franklin, Tennessee 37067. Manuscripts will be returned if a self-addressed stamped envelope is included.